This book is for individuals
who are going through
a difficult time recovering
from a broken heart
and seeking serenity, growth,
and positivity.

**You will GROW through
what you GO through.**

I love you.

Relationships are
harder now because

EVERYONE WANTS
THE IDEA OF LOVE

but **cannot commit
to the substance**.

You **can't**
have peace
with someone
who isn't

at PEACE
with THEMSELVES.

The wait and healing are necessary.

When it's your turn,
you'll look back
and realize
that the time spent
with God, healing,
and self-care
was all worth it.

All we want is to be loved
by someone who has

A GENUINE HEART,

genuine intentions,
genuine affection,
and **genuine purpose**.

It is not worth it to
stay in a relationship
because you love someone.

LOVE ISN'T ENOUGH.

Reassurance, communication,
attention, affection, time,
satisfaction, and someone
who can emotionally connect
with you are all important.

Let's normalize
letting go
of people who **repeatedly break our heart.**

WALK AWAY

if you don't feel
loved, appreciated,
desired, needed,
or as if you belong!

IT IS IMPORTANT THAT YOU ARE HAPPY.

There's no need to
pretend to love someone
you don't love just
because they could change.

**When your present
is a tragedy, don't wait
for their potential.**

Not to spoil the ending, but

You WILL HEAL AT THE END.

Remember that.

Date to marry.
Court to marry.
Invest to marry.
Commit to marry.

No one has time to be
playing house and
doing this on and off
relationship mess that's
getting them nowhere.

Love with commitment,
not with confusion.

I pray you

DON'T RUN BACK TO WHAT'S TOXIC

because you're
afraid of being alone.

**Stop hurting
innocent people**
because you
refuse to heal.

If you're broken,
relationships
aren't for you,

healing is.

LOVE YOURSELF
ENOUGH

to stop seeking
a reason why they left you.

The answer won't
help you move on.

But choosing you will.

I don't know who needs this,
but you need to delete
their contact and block them.

If you're still answering,
peeking, sneaking, texting,
and checking up on them,
you'll never move on.

DO WHAT'S BEST FOR YOU.

Even if that means coming out
of your comfort zone.

Sometimes you have to
forgive people who aren't sorry.

Sometimes you have to
move on without closure.

Sometimes the person you want
doesn't deserve you.

Sometimes
being single is your best option.

Sometimes you need to
let go and get yourself together.

IT ISN'T EASY,
BUT IT'S WORTH IT.

stop letting unprepared people waste your time.

You're not someone
who wants seasonal love or
someone to pass time with.

You want to date and
marry with purpose.

You expect real commitment.

But entertaining clowns won't
prosper your purpose.

THAT BREAKUP
WAS THE PEACE
YOU'VE BEEN
PRAYING FOR.

**Sleeping with a broken heart
isn't easy.**

So I empathize with those
who struggle to sleep at night
while trying to find peace.

But understand this,
Joy comes in the morning.
Pray, read, and listen to
some empowering music.

THIS IS THE SEASON YOU SURVIVE AND THRIVE!

**Someday you'll realize
that it wasn't your fault.**
There was nothing
you could have done
to make them love you,
appreciate you, act right,
behave, choose you,
stop cheating,
or take accountability
for their actions.

You did the right thing.

It hurts.
But you did the right thing.

You'll miss them,
you'll want to call them,
you'll want to reach out,
and you'll even want closure.

But never forget the
disrespect, the dishonesty,
the unloyalty, and the lack of
communication when

ALL YOU WANTED WAS LOVE.

YOU CAN'T BE FRIENDS WITH THOSE WHO BROKE YOUR HEART,

ruined your life,
took advantage of your love,
kindness, and forgiveness.
**They don't deserve
access to your life.**
There is no friendship there.
So, no, you can't wish them
a happy birthday.
Be thankful for your own birth.

They're sleeping and you're crying.
You are hurt, you want revenge,
you want them to hurt as much as you do,
and **you want closure and answers.**
I get it, but you will not receive closure
in every situation.

Some connections are better off disconnected.

FUN FACT:

you don't need anyone
to complete you.

YOU ARE WHOLE
BY YOURSELF.

Keep shining in
your singleness.

HEALING
NEGOT

IS NOT

IABLE.

If your ex moved on quickly,
and found somebody else.
That's their business.

You move on and

FIND YOURSELF.

What they're doing and
who they're doing it with
is **none of your business**.

Don't let

your loneliness

make you reconnect
with **toxic people**.

You'll miss them until
you don't anymore.

Stop blaming yourself

and *START*
HEALING.

Whatever you do...

DON'T LOSE FAITH IN LOVE

because some **vows don't break**,
some **commitments last forever**,
some **desires don't expire**,
and some
connections don't separate.

NOT EVERYONE YOU LOSE *is a* LOSS.

**Some breakups
are meant to bring you**

CLOSER TO
GOD.

Some relationships
didn't work out for a reason.

BE THANKFUL
GOD WOKE YOU UP

before they broke you.

No matter how much you miss them,
please don't contact them.

You deserve happiness.

and going back to what broke you
doesn't encourage change,
it delays peace.

I hope this time
when you see the red flags,
you don't ignore them.

I hope this time
when you see the lack of effort,

*you don't force it
or try to change them.*

you pack up and go.

I pray that you

Never

LOOK BACK,
GO BACK,
or **CALL BACK**

those who don't deserve you.

My heart breaks for anyone
who lays in bed at night and
wonders why they weren't
good enough for the one person
they would give the world to.

But here's the truth,
it's better to break your own heart
by walking away than
sticking around where
love doesn't exist.

BE STRONG!

There are times
when you have to
let go and move on.

To save yourself.

To save your children.

TO SAVE YOUR LIFE.

**No exceptions,
just freedom.**

It hurts when they
move on so quickly.
And act as if they're happy
with someone else and
you never mattered.

Don't fall for it.

Some people try to find love
to shadow pain.

You focus on *healing,*
growing, and *winning.*

Don't let loneliness force you
into a relationship you have
no business being in.

**Never blame yourself
when someone else hurts you.**
Sometimes you can't control
how they treat you, or even how
they treat themselves.
And truth is, their behavior
doesn't mean you're
not good enough.

IT MEANS
YOU DESERVE BETTER.

You can't fall in love
with an empty person
and expect them
to fulfill your needs.

Some relationships need to end.
And you need to realize
when they don't love you,

THEY JUST LOVE
THE WAY
YOU LOVE THEM.

I know it hurts.

I know you feel like
you weren't good enough.

BUT YOUR

BREAKTHROUGH

IS COMING.

Don't give up on yourself now.
You came too far.
Your value is still high
and you're still beautiful.
**You don't need anyone
to claim you to feel whole.
Let it hurt and grow from it.**

I am so incredibly proud
of people who pull themselves
out of toxic situations and relationships.

It takes so much courage and
strength to stand up to an abuser
and say

Enough is enough.

I am so proud of you.

Being single is better than being
taken advantage of, cheated on,
lied to, abused, with a narcissist, put down,
and around someone who
really doesn't know how to love you
or even love themselves.

STAY SINGLE
UNTIL YOU'RE APPRECIATED.

Stop stressing over people
who aren't stressing over you.
Stop wasting your valuable time
and energy chasing people
who don't want to be caught.

**If they aren't for you
then they aren't for you.**

Don't raise your blood pressure...

*raise your
standards!*

STOP BEING LOYAL TO YOUR PAIN.

They were no good for you.

They created the circumstances and then played victim.
They invaded your life with promises and flattery
but produced nothing but pain and lies.

Understand this, you will never reach royalty
if you're still attached to the village idiot.

Some people are really messed up,
and it's **not your job to fix them.**

DON'T GO CRAZY TRYING TO CHANGE SOMEONE WHO LIKES BEING A MESS.

Sometimes you have to accept the fact
that some people are who they are.
And you're better off alone than
trying to fix people you didn't break.

FORGIVENESS
DOESN'T REQUIRE
RECONNECTING.

God
is restoring
all the years
you wasted
with the wrong person.

Stop wasting your time
on those who can't commit
to your love language.

Those who don't take
your feelings into consideration
or respect your opinion.

TRUTH IS,
IF SOMEONE ISN'T FOR YOU...
THEY AREN'T FOR YOU.

Stop recycling the wrong person.

NOT ONLY DOES GOD
REPLACE WHAT YOU'VE LOST,
HE UPGRADES IT.

**Someone desiring you
is not the same
as someone valuing you.**
Don't entertain them
if they aren't willing
to put in the effort to create
an amazing relationship.

GO WHERE
YOU'RE VALUED.

I

LOVE

YOU.

CPSIA information can be obtained
at www.ICGtesting.com
Printed in the USA
LVHW072007021121
702218LV00007B/144